Zoom In on Materials

Plastic

Andrea Rivera

abdopublishing.com

Published by Abdo Zoom™, PO Box 398166, Minneapolis, Minnesota 55439. Copyright © 2018 by Abdo Consulting Group, Inc. International copyrights reserved in all countries. No part of this book may be reproduced in any form without written permission from the publisher. Abdo Zoom™ is a trademark and logo of Abdo Consulting Group, Inc.

Printed in the United States of America, North Mankato, Minnesota
052017
092017

Cover Photo: Olena Rublenko/iStockphoto
Interior Photos: Olena Rublenko/iStockphoto, 1; Miguel Malo/iStockphoto, 4; Shutterstock Images, 5, 10, 11, 17; iStockphoto, 6, 8–9, 13, 16–17, 21; Abbie Images/iStockphoto, 7; Andre Penner/AP Images, 14; Teerasak Ladnongkhun/Shutterstock Images, 18

Editor: Brienna Rossiter
Series Designer: Madeline Berger
Art Direction: Dorothy Toth

Publishers Cataloging-in-Publication Data
Names: Rivera, Andrea, author.
Title: Plastic / by Andrea Rivera.
Description: Minneapolis, MN : Abdo Zoom, 2018. | Series: Materials |
    Includes bibliographical references and index.
Identifiers: LCCN 2017931136 | ISBN 9781532120336 (lib. bdg.) |
    ISBN 9781614797449 (ebook) | ISBN 9781614798002 (Read-to-me ebook)
Subjects: LCSH: Plastics--Juvenile literature.
Classification: DDC 668.4--dc23
LC record available at http://lccn.loc.gov/2017931136

Table of Contents

Plastic is a material.
It is made from
resins.

The resins are melted.
Plastic forms.

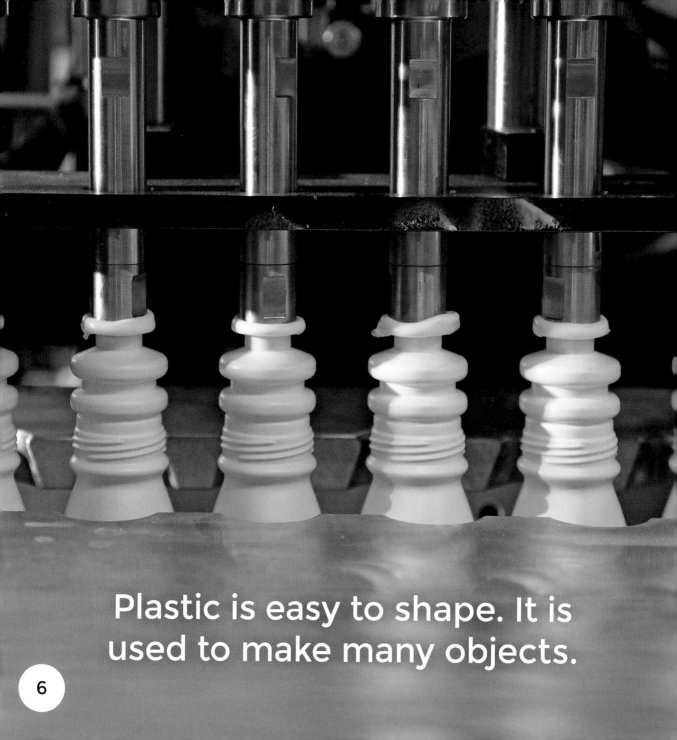

Plastic is easy to shape. It is used to make many objects.

Bottles and bags are often made from plastic.

Some resins have chemicals added to them before they are made into plastic.

The chemicals can make the plastic stronger. Some make it stretchy. Others change its color.

Melted plastic can be shaped.
It is poured into a **mold**.

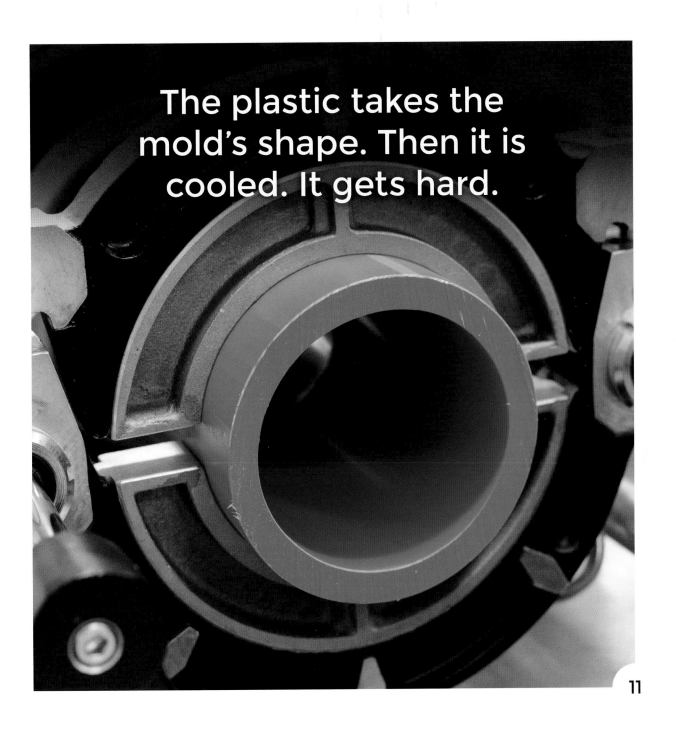

The plastic takes the mold's shape. Then it is cooled. It gets hard.

Some plastic can be **recycled**. Machines break it into pieces. Ovens melt the pieces. The pieces are made into beads. The beads are used to make other things.

Art

Throwing away plastic can hurt the earth. An artist from Brazil made sculptures. They looked like big plastic bottles. He put them by a river. They reminded people to recycle.

Math

Used plastic is sent to landfills.
It breaks down into dirt.

This takes a long time.
Plastic bags can take
20 years to break down.

Plastic bottles take 450 years to break down. Reusing plastic is better for the earth.

Key Stats

- People in the United States use more than 100 billion plastic bags each year.

- Plastic is light. It is often used to hold food or drinks.

- Less than 0.25 pounds (0.11 kg) of plastic can hold a gallon of milk.

- Plastic is also used to make electronic devices, machine parts, and appliances.

Glossary

landfill - a place where trash is buried between layers of dirt.

mold - a hollow form used to shape something.

recycled - used again or used to make something new.

resins - pellets or powder made by joining many molecules together.

sculpture - an art form (such as a statue) that is three-dimensional, not flat.

Booklinks

For more information on plastic,
please visit abdobooklinks.com

Zoom In on STEAM!

Learn even more with the Abdo Zoom
STEAM database. Check out
abdozoom.com for more information.

Index